W9-CHR-470

636.39   Wood, ALix
WOO   Pygmy goats

DATE DUE			
FEB 2 3 2010			
JAN 1 9 2011			

MINI ANIMALS

Pygmy Goats

by Alix Wood

WINDMILL BOOKS

New York

Published in 2017 by **Windmill Books**, An Imprint of Rosen Publishing
29 East 21st Street, New York, NY 10010

Editor: Eloise Macgregor
Designer: Alix Wood
Consultant: Jean Sisco, Chair of the Publications Committee of the National Pygmy
    Goat Association

Photo Credits: Cover, 1 © AdobeStock; 4 © Glen Bowman; 5 © Michael Westhoff/iStock; 6 © Shutterstock; 7 © Dr Asamoah Larbi; 8 © Stuart Caie; 9 © Toshihiro Gamo; 10-11, 14 © Shutterstock; 12, 20, 28 © The Big WRanch12; 13 © WindRanch; 15 © Malachi Jacobs/Shutterstock; 16 © Ralph Daily; 17 © Jeff Stanford; 18 © Gabe Taviano; 19 left all © Henry Williams; 19 right © Armin Kübelbeck; 21 © SashaFoxWalters/iStock; 22 © Dreamstime; 23 © JoePhoto; 24 © Jmkarohl; 25 © Jen Grantham/iStock; 26 © Dave Wilcock; 27 left © AdobeStock; 27 right © JamBox998; 29 © Mark Peters Photography

Cataloging-in-Publication Data
Names: Wood, Alix.
Title: Pygmy goats / Alix Wood.
Description: New York : Windmill Books, 2017. | Series: Mini animals| Includes index.
Identifiers: ISBN 9781499481648 (pbk.) | ISBN 9781499481655 (library bound) | ISBN
    9781508192992 (6 pack)
Subjects: LCSH: Goats--Juvenile literature.
Classification: LCC SF383.35 W66 2017 | DDC 636.3'9--dc23

Manufactured in the United States of America
CPSIA Compliance Information: Batch #: BW17PK. For Further Information contact: Windmill Books, New York, New York at 1-866-478-0556

Contents

Friendly Pygmy Goats

Pygmy goats are a very small breed of goat. Adults measure between 16-23 inches (41-58 cm) tall at the shoulders. That's around half the height of a regular goat! Pygmy goats may be small but they are full of character. They are smart and very friendly.

Pygmy goats are fun animals to watch. They are very playful. They like to jump and chase each other. They love to climb, too. These two young baby Pygmy goats have some logs that they can climb in their enclosure.

Cute Alert!

All goats are good at escaping. Pygmy goats are very good at escaping! They need strong fences to keep them in.

5

Where Do Pygmy Goats Come From?

You can find Pygmy goats all over the world nowadays. Originally, most breeds came from West Africa. There were several different breeds, such as the African Pygmy goat, the Nigerian Dwarf goat, and the Sudanese Pygmy goat.

Pygmy goats come mainly from Nigeria and the Cameroon Valley area, marked in red on this map. The Sudanese Pygmy goat came from Southern Sudan, marked in purple on the map. The different breeds are now usually all simply known as Pygmy goats.

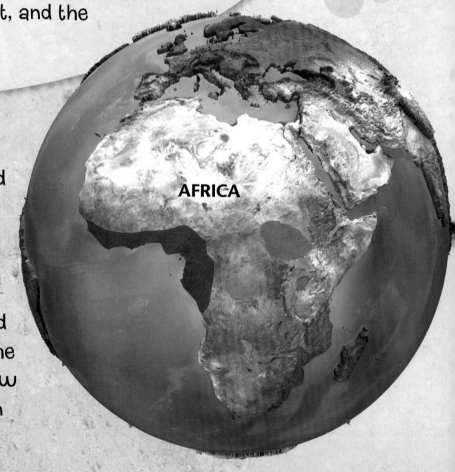

AFRICA

It is thought that Pygmy goats became small as a result of the conditions in the warm, wet forests of West and Central Africa. Being small must have been a benefit. Perhaps being small meant they needed less food, or they could hide from predators more easily.

In West Africa, people have kept Pygmy goats for thousands of years. They are kept for their milk and meat.

Males and Females

A male Pygmy goat is called a **buck**. A female goat is called a **doe**. Does are considered easier to keep than bucks. Bucks are larger, and can give off an unpleasant smell during the **mating** season.

Cute Alert!

This Pygmy goat buck looks very cute. Bucks can be quite aggressive though. His long horns would hurt if this buck **butted** you.

Both male and female Pygmy goats have horns. The doe pictured above has had her horns taken off. People who own Pygmy goats will often take off their animals' horns. This keeps them from getting their heads stuck in fences and feeders. It also prevents them from hurting other animals.

Pygmy Goat Pets

Pygmy goats are becoming very popular as pets. Because the goats are small, they are not too expensive to feed. Their size also makes them easier to handle and transport than most other **livestock**.

Before getting a Pygmy goat, you need to check that you are legally allowed to keep them where you live. Some areas do not allow people to keep goats. In other areas, you may need a special **license**.

Pygmy goats were first brought to the United States in the late 1950s. At first they were mainly kept in zoos. They were so friendly and fun to watch that people began to want to keep Pygmy goats.

Goats are naturally curious. They like the company of people and will want to spend time with their owners. They make great companions.

Cute Alert!
Pygmy goats will often wag their tail when they are happy, just like a dog does!

Nigerian Dwarf Goats

Nigerian Dwarf goats come from Nigeria in West Africa. Whereas most African Pygmy goats are raised for their meat, the Nigerian Dwarf goat is a miniature **dairy** goat, which means it is kept for its milk.

Cute Alert!

Nigerian Dwarf goats come in many different colors. They are usually a mixture of white, black, chocolate, or gold.

12

Most Nigerian Dwarf goats have blue eyes. If a Pygmy goat has blue eyes it is not considered to be a pure Pygmy goat. The goat probably has a Nigerian Dwarf goat somewhere in their family background.

Like many **prey** animals, goats have **horizontal** slit-shaped pupils. This shape allows the goats to see in virtually all directions at once. This helps the goats keep a watch out for **predators**.

Tiny Baby Goats

A Pygmy goat doe carries her young for around 5 months. They usually have one or two babies, but they can occasionally have three. Newborn goats are called **kids**. Tiny baby Pygmy goats are super cute!

Cute Alert!

Baby Pygmy goats are born covered in hair. They can get up and walk just a few minutes after being born.

Pygmy goats are **mammals**. Mammals' young drink milk from their mothers. A doe that is feeding her young may need extra food so she can produce plenty of milk.

A Home for a Pygmy Goat

The most important thing a Pygmy goat needs is company. They do not like to live alone. Many Pygmy goat breeders will not sell just one goat to people, unless they are sure there are more goats already at the buyer's home.

This enclosure is perfect for Pygmy goats. The goats have company. The enclosure has strong fencing, and the goats have logs to climb on.

Pygmy goats will graze on a pasture. During winter, or if they don't have a pasture, they need good quality grass or hay. Goats need fresh, clean water and a salt block for them to lick. Goats love vegetables and fruit, too. Pygmy goats love to snack on twigs, leaves, bark, and even weeds! Pregnant and nursing does and young kids may need extra goat feed.

Some common plants, trees, and flowers are poisonous to goats. Owners need an expert to check their pasture, and give advice on which plants are bad for their goats.

Caring for Pygmy Goats

Pygmy goats need a little care to keep them healthy. Their **hooves** need trimming every few weeks. Overgrown hooves can be uncomfortable. Pygmy goats can get worms. Worms are a **parasite** that will make the goats unwell. Worming medicine given around twice a year should prevent this.

Cute Alert!

Goats really don't like getting wet. If you need to bathe your goat, it's best to get them used to water when very young.

Goat Grooming

Grooming a Pygmy goat is important. It helps keep the goat's coat healthy and free from **lice**. It's also a good time to check over your goat for any injuries.

1 Use a hard brush to get any surface mud and dirt off.

hard brush

2 Next, use a curry comb to help loosen any hidden dirt.

curry comb

3 Rub the goat with a soft brush to oil the goat's coat. They love the massage.

soft brush

4 It is best for an adult to clip a goat's hooves. The clippers are sharp.

hoof clippers

Useful Companions

Because Pygmy goats are so friendly, they get along with most other animals. They always want to play and make friends. Pygmy goats also get along well with people. Their owners sometimes take Pygmy goats into hospitals or nursing homes. Their cuteness and love of life helps cheer up the residents.

Almost all animals like a Pygmy goat's company. This kid is making friends with a pet cat.

Cute Alert!

Horse owners will often use some Pygmy goats to keep a lonely horse company.

Pygmy goats
and horses easily
become friends.
Pygmy goats have been
known to ride around on horses' backs!

The main problem with keeping a Pygmy in with a horse is making sure that their field is secure. Not only do you need to keep the Pygmy goat in, it is also important to keep animals that might prey on the goats out. Coyotes and stray dogs have been known to kill Pygmy goats.

Pygmy Goat Gardeners

Pygmy goats have been known to eat just about anything. If you have ever been to a petting zoo and met a goat you have probably seen this. They will eat the goat food you give them, and then they usually also eat the bag the food was in! Once they have finished that, they will probably start eating your clothes!

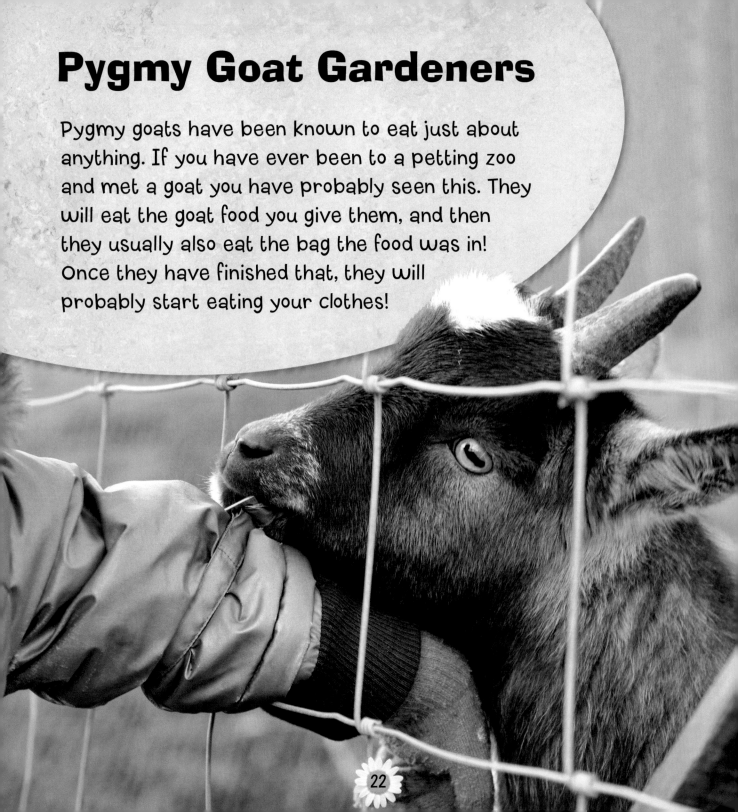

Pygmy goat owners can use their goat's amazing appetite. Pygmy goats are often used to clear scrubland. They make great garden helpers, as long as they don't get in a vegetable or flower garden—they would destroy it!

Goats don't make good lawn mowers, however. Unlike sheep, who will happily graze a lawn, goats are **browsers**, not grazers. That means they eat higher leaves, shoots, and fruits. Grazers such as sheep feed on grass or other low **vegetation**.

Cute Alert!
Pygmy goats can be quite fussy about eating off the floor. They will usually only eat their hay if it is put in a feeder on the wall.

Pygmy Goats Give Milk

Female Pygmy goats produce milk for their young. They provide milk for around a year after giving birth, so many goat owners get to have some milk, too. Pygmy goat milk is sweet and tastes delicious. Does usually produce around a half gallon (2.3 liters) of milk per day.

You can make cheese and ice cream from Pygmy goat milk. The high **butterfat** milk makes great moisturizing soap bars, too!

This Nigerian Dwarf goat has an udder full of tasty milk.

It is an art to milk a Pygmy goat by hand. Give the doe some food to keep her happy. Pet her to make her relaxed. Make sure you feel relaxed, too. Clean and **sterilize** the udders and bucket. Wrap your thumb and forefinger around a teat to trap some milk inside. Squeeze your middle finger, then your ring finger, and then your pinky to squirt out the milk. Relax your grip to allow milk to fill the teat again.

Cute Alert!

One of the problems with milking Pygmy goats is that they are pretty close to the floor. Milking stands like this one help raise the goats up a little!

At the Showground

Some Pygmy goat owners enter their animals into shows. It can be fun to meet other owners and show off your pet. Owners can make new friends and learn from each other.

It's not easy to persuade a buck to behave in the show ring. Owners should practice walking their goats using a leash before the big day.

Before the show, owners need to clean and brush their goat's coat, and trim their hooves. They should practice getting the goat to stand calmly while the judge looks them over, too.

You can enter a Pygmy goat into classes depending on their age. Different countries have different classes and standards. If a goat doesn't have an official **pedigree**, it can be entered into pet classes. Young handlers can also win prizes. There are usually classes for handlers aged between 5 and 10, and between 11 and 16. It's fun to win a ribbon.

Test Your Knowledge

1. Where did Pygmy goats originally come from?
   a) Australia b) West Africa c) the West Indies

2. What is a baby goat called?
   a) a buck b) a doe c) a kid

3. Both male and female goats have horns.
   a) true b) false

4. Why do Pygmy goats have slit-shaped pupils?
   a) to help them see in color
   b) to help them see in many directions at once
   c) to make them look cute

5. What does a mother goat feed her kids?
   a) milk b) hay c) weeds

6 Why should you never buy just one Pygmy goat?
a) because they are so cheap
b) because they need company

7 What can you use Pygmy goat milk for?
a) making cheese b) making ice cream
c) making soap d) all of the above

8 Which of these uses are Pygmy goats great for?
a) lawn mowing
b) clearing weeds and scrub
c) helping in the vegetable garden

How did you do? The answers are on page 32.

Glossary

browsers Animals that have a diet of leaves.

buck A male goat.

butted Hit with the head or horns.

butterfat The natural fat in milk and dairy products.

dairy Animals used for producing milk.

doe A female goat.

hooves A covering of horn that protects the toes of some mammals.

horizontal Parallel to the horizon.

kids A goat's young.

lice A wingless parasite that lives on warm-blooded animals.

license Permission granted by a qualified authority.

livestock Farm animals.

mammals Warm-blooded animals that have a backbone and hair, breathe air, and feed milk to their young.

mating Coming together to create young.

parasite A living thing that lives in or on another living thing.

pedigree A recorded pure breed animal.

predators An animal that lives by killing and eating other animals.

prey An animal hunted or killed by another animal for food.

sterilize To rid of germs.

vegetation Plant life.

Further Information

Books

Duffee, Alice. *Toga the Goat*. Victoria, Canada: FriesenPress, 2016.

Emerson, Joan. *Scholastic Reader Level 2: Teensy Weensy Animals*. New York, NY: Scholastic Paperbacks, 2015.

Rudick, Dina. *Barnyard Kids: A Family Guide for Raising Animals*. Beverly, MA: Quarry Books, 2015.

Websites

For web resources related to the subject of this book, go to: **www.windmillbooks.com/weblinks** and select this book's title.

Index

Answers 1) b, 2) c, 3) a, 4) b, 5) a, 6) b, 7) d, 8) b